RULES TO RULE IN BUSINESS

STRATEGIES TO INCREASE EFFICIENCY AND ACHIEVE COST REDUCTION FASTER

RULES TO RULE IN BUSINESS

Strategies to Increase Efficiency and Achieve Cost Reduction Faster

"Efficiency Step-up Blueprint" **Explained in** step-by-step ready to implement process

Also introducing the "5 Power Principles" of Highly Efficient Manufacturing Units:

- Superior Output
- Zero Firefighting
- No Replacements
- Minimum Rejections
- Maximum Productivity

Jai Sethi

Business Efficiency Architect

Inventor of Efficiency Step-up Blueprint

RULES TO RULE IN BUSINESS

STRATEGIES TO
INCREASE EFFICIENCY AND ACHIEVE
COST REDUCTION FASTER

Achieve Maximum Efficiency with
Lesser Resources

Decoding the Japanese Manufacturers'
Secrets with easy implementable Steps

By

Jai Sethi

Business Efficiency Architect

Inventor of Efficiency Step-up Blueprint

Worldwide Published by
Pendown Press

PENDOWN PRESS LLP
An ISO 9001 & ISO 14001 Certified Co.,
Regd. Office: 3767A, Kanhaiya Nagar,
Tri Nagar, Delhi-110035
Ph.: 8130886000, 9650072927, 8595249536
E-mail: info@pendownpress.com
Branch Office: 1A/2A, 20, Hari Sadan, Ansari Road,
Daryaganj, New Delhi-110002
Ph.: 011-45794768
Website: PendownPress.com

First Edition: 2024
Price: ₹ 349/-
ISBN: 978-93-7217-953-8

Layout and Cover Designed by Pendown Graphics Team
Printed and Bound in India by Thomson Press India Ltd.

Table of Contents

Section 1
Background

My Story

This is no coincidence!

Hello, my name is Jai Sethi, I am a Business Efficiency Architect and Management Coach. My tryst with Business Efficiency and its relationship with Business Growth began early on, in my career, nineteen years back.

When as a chartered accountant, I started doing internal audits and began observing the plant operations of several manufacturing units and noticed the gaps in the production processes of Indian manufacturers. Since Japanese manufacturers have an enormous repute for their high level of productivity, I started reading and observing their theories & practices, and I also started comparing these processes and practices with the ones being followed in Indian manufacturing units.

Ever since the start of my career and throughout my journey, I have always been mesmerized by lots of concepts that these Japanese manufacturers have been following. Despite the fact that some aspects of these are particular to the Japanese culture and economy, the Japanese system is widely recognized as delivering many of the efficiencies and cost reductions it sets out to.

I have played a key role in implementing these concepts to many Indian manufacturers and improved their productivity, reduced their costs, and thereby improved their profitability to an extraordinary level.

I live and breathe process improvements daily, and they continue to top my mind; so that I may deliver measurable results on a consistent basis.

The journey so far has been brilliant!

I'm sure you must be wondering why I'm sharing all these concepts in an integrated manner in complete detail through this book when I could have charged a premium for sharing the information on a piecemeal basis.

After all, if you implement the suggestions shared in this book, you can easily make a highly efficient manufacturing setup and grow your business in leaps and bounds.

Besides, the often heard & learned business parlance, that, " There is no free lunch" must also be playing on your mind.

So why this book?

One, being in love with processes, it breaks my heart to see how manufacturers waste their resources on inefficient processes. That's why I want to guide maximum manufacturing facilities onto the right path.

Two, I am unable to coach everyone personally due to time constraints, so this book is my gift to all manufacturers to share the 5 Power Principles and my self-developed innovative and practical "Efficiency Step-up Blueprint" that I have observed, researched and learnt during my journey as a Business Growth Consultant.

I am sure these lessons will steer you onto the path of being more and more efficient and profitable as a result. So, without further ado, let's explore the 5 Power Principles I learnt about Process Efficiency...

Your own "Business Efficiency Architect"
– Jai Sethi

P.S.

1. *As the "Efficiency Step-up Blueprint" is a very deep concept it requires thorough understanding before you start implementing it. Any doubts or queries you wish to address on the same are welcome on this mail id jai@jaise t h i.co m*
2. *Although this "Efficiency Step-up Blueprint" was initially developed keeping manufacturing set-ups in mind; however, in my own experiences, it has worked equally great for service organizations as well.*
3. *The only caution a business owner must keep in mind while implementing these concepts are the 3 'C's*
   a. *Consistency*
   b. *Clarity, and*
   c. *Commitment*

So that efficiency becomes the "Culture" of the Organization.

I have shared all the core concepts in an easy-to-do format in this book and I am sure these will prove to be of immense value to you. I'd love to hear how you overcome your efficiency challenges and improve the productivity and profitability of the organization. and how this book helped you in meeting the goals of your manufacturing business.

Do share your experiences here with me at

jai@jaise t h i.co m.

Your Goal Card

Write your top 3 "Goals" here as you start reading this Book.

1.

2.

3.

And I'd also love to hear your feedback about the understanding & implementation of the principles and the framework shared in this Book.

Your success stories will motivate me to tweak and make this model even more valuable going ahead.

Challenges I Observed

Time is money

We all know this and feel it from the heart, but do we really live and work by it?

In the long run, the success and profitability of your business depends upon your efficiency. The greater efficiency you can ensure, the more profitable your business will be. Despite the fact that most business owners understand this basic principle they still face various challenges in enhancing their efficiency.

Indian manufacturers need to overcome various internal challenges and need to change their style in dealing with the uncertainties of the market. Businesses that have multiple locations also need to work out a system with their vendors and channel partners across regions. They could face challenges relating to communication and coordination that would impact their productivity and ultimately could hurt their profitability.

Let us take a look at the key challenges that Indian manufacturers normally face.

1. **Inefficient Processes**

   Whether we consciously design or not, a repeated pattern of activity will become a process. Indian businesses are known for developing processes with time instead of consciously designing them as per need. This is a very long & unprofessional style, and it is a wastage of time and resources significantly.

Businesses with unplanned and outdated processes can never result in a productive environment at the workplace. Even a lack of a clear continuous improvement strategy impacts productivity in business adversely.

2. Weak Time Management

It is no secret that the success of a business is the function of its ability to manage its time. Many manufacturers suffer from time management issues. Lack of proper scheduling and lack of production planning brings a high negative impact on the operational efficiency of the business.

3. Poor Organizational Communication

Complex hierarchy and unplanned organizational structure make communication challenging and sometimes totally ineffective. This brings ambiguity in communication and confusion among employees. Inability to convey the intended messages and unclear reporting structures makes internal control weak and ultimately business suffers from low productivity.

4. Not Focusing on Training

Most Indian businesses feel that employee training on the business processes is unnecessary, and the employees can acquire required skills on the job, but this notion is not correct. Businesses with untrained employees waste their time and efforts on either assisting their team or reworking on the assigned job. This hurts productivity and the quality of output severely.

The Learnings I Took

Post-World War II era, when Japan had surrendered, and the Japanese army was completely disarmed. Japanese manufacturers started recruiting army personnel in large numbers. And because of this defence-dominated mindset with a growth-hungry corporate league, a new fusion of management techniques emerged, and this new Japanese school of management came into practice. These influential practices and philosophies reached the height of their prominence in the 1980s.

All these new techniques and different models of productivity improvement of Japanese manufacturers; made their way to worldwide manufacturing operations. These Japanese manufacturers were not only more profitable, but their distinguishing characteristics were an emphasis on designing processes to optimize efficiency and a strong commitment to quality.

Perhaps the most widely recognized collection of Japanese manufacturing techniques is what is known as the Toyota Production System (TPS), the core of which is the just-in-time (JIT) production or so-called lean manufacturing.

The pioneers of these methods were Taiichi Ohno, a former Toyota executive, and Shigeo Shingo, an eminent engineer and consultant. In his 1989 book The Study of the Toyota Production System from an Industrial Engineering Perspective, Shingo identified these basic features of TPS.

The major Characteristics of this Lean Production System that I have identified are.

1. Cost reductions by eliminating waste (whether it is staff time, materials, or other resources).
2. Reducing the likelihood of overproduction by maintaining low inventories and minimal manpower.
3. Reducing the production cycle time significantly with innovations like the Single-Minute Exchange of Die (SMED) system, which cuts downtime and enables small-lot production.
4. Order-based production; by aligning the sales team and production planning.

These newer practices were in contrast to the traditional practices of Western manufacturers, which emphasized mass production, full capacity utilization, and the economies of scale that were presumed to follow.

This book and my 5 Power Principles revolve around the core philosophies of Japanese Manufacturers that have been widely followed by them. They've also been helping their suppliers & vendors to follow these techniques so that their counterparts also help them in achieving the maximum efficiencies.

The 4 key factors

Efficiency has 4 key factors that should be focused on to improve. All the process improvement efforts should aim to improve these to enhance the performance of the operations.

These key factors are very crucial to improving the efficiency and productivity of the business.

They are:

1. Quality
2. Quantity
3. Cost
4. Time

These four parameters will become your first performance measurement criteria.

The Game of Excellence in Business

Begins here...

The Discovery

The "Efficiency Step-up Blueprint"

A manufacturer should focus on different aspects of their business separately to improve the process efficiency of their manufacturing facility. I mean that you should take a holistic approach to production by considering every element of your process, from planning and resource optimization to personnel management and quality control.

I have developed this innovative and powerful "Efficiency Step-up Blueprint" as detailed below, that takes care of everything and can give magical results.

Whether your efforts & focus are required towards automation or process optimization, development of key metrics and data insights, accelerating product innovation cycles, improving customer experience and engagement strategies, optimizing costs through waste reduction initiatives, developing talent management plans for long-term success, or leveraging external partnerships for growth opportunities along with measuring performance; whatever facet of efficiency enhancement you can think of, this framework will take care of every aspect.

You should be focusing on each individual area; one at a time rather than trying to tackle them all at once.

As a manufacturer, you should ensure that your processes are running as efficiently as possible for maximum output in the long run. Working on these individual pieces will create a comprehensive strategy that can help a business achieve maximum output while maintaining efficient operations.

This efficiency step-up blueprint takes care of all aspects and gives you a systematic intervention plan to gradually improve your productivity to achieve your goals of organizational success & profitability.

The Blueprint

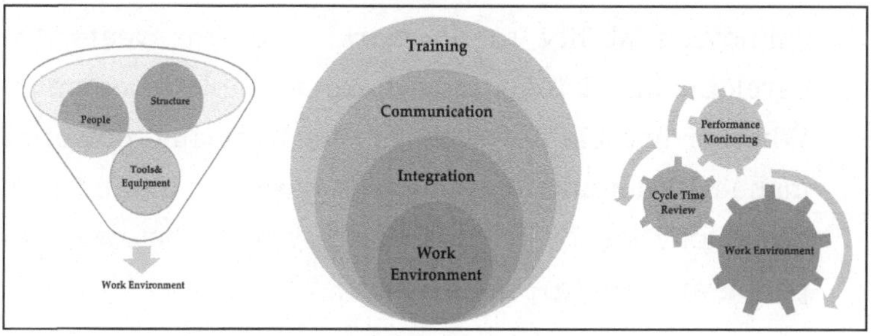

This Blueprint has 3 parts

1. Creating a Work Environment
2. Speeding up the Work Environment
3. Enhancing Effectiveness of the Work Environment

Let us dissect each part separately and go deeper into the concept.

A Work Environment in any business consists of 3 parts.

1. **Structure**

   Arrangement, grouping or processes of interrelated elements. It will include instructions, processes, documentation & hierarchy etc.

2. **People**

   Finding the right people in a team with the right mix of professional skills; associated in the right hierarchy and aligned rightly with the goals of the organization.

3. **Tools & Equipment**

   A tool is an instrument that increases an employee's ability to do work. Over the years, the development of tools moved from simple to complex. Whether muscle-powered or mechanically powered, manual or automatic, technology-based, or intelligence-based, physical or process-based system whatever your people are using to create output.

Once an organization has developed a basic work environment and ensures that it has started working; it should start working on phase 2 of speeding up the Work environment.

Speeding up must be done in the following three ways.

Although it doesn't have to be in any specific order but still all these three ways are desired to be focused on with equal intensity.

These are:

1. **Training**

An initiative consisting of educational activities within an organization that are designed to improve the job performance of an individual or group. These programs are usually focused on advancing a worker's knowledge and skill sets and instilling greater motivation to enhance job performance. Common training practices include orientations, classroom lectures, case studies, role playing, simulations and computer-based training, including e-learning etc.

2. **Communication**

Strategic communication that engages employees in the company's purpose, mission and values can increase the speed at which an organization achieves its goals. It can educate, motivate, inspire, and increase employee engagement. High employee engagement leads to better customer experience, productivity, retention, and profitability, which are all metrics that affect an organization's success.

3. **Integration**

Integration is the process of joining software, hardware, modules, and processes into one cohesive infrastructure, enabling all pieces to work as a whole. It simply results in increased productivity. Integrated systems allow centralized control over the daily processes, which adds to the efficiency of the entire workflow. A company gets more work done in less time due to the fact that employees can use all apps, data, information & tools they need from one entry point. It also avoids duplicity of work.

Phase 2 of speeding up the work environment is a continuous process, and the objective is to grow the efficiency wheel as much as we can. However, a monthly/quarterly review of the whole work environment is essential.

Here comes phase 3 of our "Efficiency Scale-up Blueprint". Phase 3 has 2 aspects of the review.

These are:

1. **Cycle Time Review**

   Usually, an organization's cost and efficiency is associated with the time duration it takes to repeat the same process or unit of output again & again. Cycle time review focuses on calculating and improving the operational performance of the business. To take a leap ahead of their competition, manufacturers need to find ways to reduce production time and cost to improve operating performance and product quality.

   If the reduction in cycle time is fifty per cent and work in process inventory turns twice, it causes output to increase from twenty to seventy per cent.

   As output increases, resource capacity is freed. Two major effects take place: expenses turn down, and the manufacturing firm becomes capable of producing considerably more output with fewer assets.

2. Process Performance Monitoring

Process Performance monitoring is a measure used to stimulate good performance outcomes. Performance monitoring involves the measurement of performance over time against indicators of performance or key performance indicators (KPIs).

It is a critical tool for planning, managing, and documenting data collection. It contributes to the effectiveness of performance management by assuring that comparable data will be collected on a regular and timely basis. These are essential to the operation of a credible and useful performance-based management approach.

Phase 3 focuses on increasing the effectiveness of the work environment. This is the most crucial part of the whole efficiency scale-up exercise.

I have personally implemented this "Efficiency Scale-up Blueprint" in many organisations in diverse fields. They were manufacturing, and services both kinds of organizations and my experience with both kinds of organizations has been enthralling.

We all know that implementation is the key to success. **The ultimate target of a business owner while implementing this "Efficiency Scale-Up Blueprint" should be to create the culture of efficiency within** the organization. **This is only possible through the following recipe.**

Culture = Consistency x Clarity x Commitment

Consistent actions with absolute clarity and commitment will prompt the mindset of the whole team towards efficiency, which will lead to productivity and, finally the profitability of the organization.

An inefficient business can never become the leader of the industry.

Only efficient businesses will survive and reward their stakeholders; Be it their vendors, employees, investors, or owners.

In the next section, we will be diving deep into each bit & piece of this "Efficiency Scale-up Blueprint". Let's understand them thoroughly and before we begin, I want you to give me a commitment that while reading this book you will start your journey of becoming the leader of your industry and making a super-efficient organization. I am with you on this journey,

Are you with me?

Say aloud, **"I am making this company super-efficient!"**

Yessss, that's the way to move forward...

Section 2

Creating a Work Environment

Structure

Structure refers to the way in which an organization, system, or process is organized and arranged in order to achieve specific goals. It involves creating a framework for how tasks should be carried out, and how decisions should be made.

Structure is an essential element in developing a positive and productive work environment. Some of the ways in which structure contributes to a positive work environment are as follows:

1. **Clarity and accountability:**

   A structured work environment provides clear expectations and guidelines for employees, which helps them understand their roles and responsibilities within the company. This clarity promotes accountability and allows employees to take ownership of their work, leading to better performance and results.

2. **Improved communication:**

   Structure helps to improve communication within the work environment by providing a clear framework for how information should be shared, and decision-making processes should be carried out. This reduces confusion and misunderstandings and helps to create a more efficient and effective workplace.

3. **Increased efficiency:**

   A structured work environment can increase efficiency by providing clear processes for carrying out tasks, reducing the amount of time and resources needed to complete projects. This can also help to minimize errors and rework, leading to better overall results.

4. **Improved morale and motivation:**

   A structured work environment can help to improve morale and motivation among employees by providing a sense of stability and security. When employees know what is expected of them and have clear guidelines to follow, they are more likely to feel confident in their work and motivated to perform to the best of their abilities.

5. **Better collaboration:**

   A structured work environment can also promote better collaboration among team members by providing clear processes for teamwork

   and communication. This can help to ensure that everyone is working together effectively towards a common goal.

Structure is an important component of a positive and productive work environment. By providing clarity, accountability, improved communication, increased efficiency, improved morale and motivation, and better collaboration, the structure can contribute significantly to the success of a company.

The key components of structure include

1. **Roles and responsibilities:**

   Defining the roles and responsibilities of each individual or team within the structure. This helps to ensure that everyone knows what is expected of them and that there is clarity around who is responsible for different aspects of the process.

2. **Procedures and protocols:**

   Developing procedures and protocols for carrying out tasks, making decisions, and resolving conflicts. This helps to ensure that processes are followed consistently, and everyone is working together effectively.

3. **Communication:**

   Establishing clear lines of communication, both within the organization and between different stakeholders. This helps ensure that information is shared effectively, and everyone is working towards the same goals.

4. **Hierarchy:**

   Creating a hierarchy of authority and decision-making power, which helps to ensure that decisions are made effectively, and everyone understands who is responsible for different aspects of the process.

5. **Processes and systems:**

   Developing processes and systems for carrying out tasks and making decisions. This helps to ensure that work is carried out in an efficient manner, and that everyone is working together effectively.

6. **Feedback and evaluation:**

Providing regular feedback and evaluation to help identify areas for improvement and to ensure that the structure is working effectively to achieve its goals.

By establishing a clear structure with these components, organizations can ensure that their processes are efficient, effective, and aligned with their goals. A well-structured organization is able to operate smoothly, reduce waste and inefficiencies, and achieve better results.

Developing an Effective Structure

Here are some steps you can take to develop structure in an organisation:

1. **Assess the current structure:**

   Conduct a thorough assessment of the current processes and systems in place to identify areas that need improvement. This will help you to understand what changes need to be made to establish a more structured work environment.

2. **Develop clear policies and procedures:**

   Develop clear policies and procedures for all aspects of the manufacturing process, including production, quality control, and inventory management. Ensure that all employees are trained on these policies and procedures and that they are followed consistently.

3. **Implement standard operating procedures (SOPs):**

   Develop and implement standard operating procedures (SOPs) for key processes in the manufacturing unit, such as production, inspection, and testing. This will help to ensure consistency and accuracy in the manufacturing process.

4. **Establish clear lines of communication:**

   Establish clear lines of communication within the manufacturing unit, such as regular meetings and a system for reporting progress and addressing issues. Encourage open communication and collaboration among employees and provide regular feedback to help them understand their roles and responsibilities.

5. **Implement continuous improvement methods:**

   Encourage continuous improvement by implementing methodologies such as Lean Manufacturing, Six Sigma, or Total Quality Management. These methodologies focus on reducing waste and improving efficiency, which can help to increase production and reduce costs.

6. **Measure and evaluate performance:** Regularly measure and evaluate performance to ensure that the manufacturing unit is meeting its goals and objectives. Use this information to identify areas for improvement and make changes as necessary to further develop structure and improve performance.

By following these steps, you can establish a more structured work environment in your manufacturing unit. This will help improve efficiency, increase production, and foster a positive work environment where employees feel valued and motivated to contribute to the success of the company.

People

People refer to individuals or groups of individuals who make up the organization. They may be related to the organization in many ways like employees, customers, suppliers, vendors, investors, promoters, and other stakeholders.

The relationships between people within an organization are critical to its success. Positive and productive relationships between employees, managers, and other stakeholders can help create a positive and productive work environment, improve communication, and foster collaboration and teamwork. This, in turn, can lead to better performance, increased job satisfaction, and higher levels of engagement among employees.

Some of the key benefits of positive people relationships in an organization include:

1. **Improved communication:**

   When employees have positive relationships with each other, they are more likely to communicate openly and effectively, which can lead to improved collaboration and better problem-solving.

2. **Increased employee engagement:**

   Employees who feel valued and connected to their colleagues are more likely to be engaged and committed to their work, which can lead to improved performance and higher levels of job satisfaction.

3. **Better teamwork:**

   Positive relationships between employees can help foster teamwork, collaboration, and cooperation, which can lead to more efficient and effective work processes.

4. **Enhanced creativity and innovation:**

   When employees feel comfortable and confident in their relationships with their colleagues, they are more likely to feel empowered to share their ideas and contribute to the organization's innovation and growth.

5. **Reduced conflict:**

   Positive relationships can help to reduce conflict and improve the overall workplace culture, leading to a more positive and productive work environment.

It is important for organizations to actively cultivate positive relationships among their employees by creating opportunities for employees to build connections, fostering open and honest communication, and promoting a culture of respect and inclusiveness. By doing so, organizations can create a positive and supportive work environment that can help improve employee satisfaction, performance, and overall organizational success.

It is important for organizations to actively cultivate positive relationships among their employees by creating opportunities for employees to build connections, fostering open and honest communication, and promoting a culture of respect and inclusiveness. By doing so, organizations can create a positive and supportive work environment that can help improve employee satisfaction, performance, and overall organizational success.

Employee-Centric Environment

Employees are the actual efficient drivers who bring changes. They are a critical component of any organization, as they are responsible for carrying out the day-to-day operations, delivering products or services, and contributing to the organization's success.

There are many different types of employees in an organization, including:

1. **Management:**

   Managers are responsible for overseeing the operations of the organization and making decisions that impact the direction and success of the company.

2. **Front-line employees:**

   Front-line employees are the individuals who interact directly with customers, clients, or the public and are responsible for delivering products or services to them.

3. **Support staff:**

   Support staff includes individuals who provide administrative, operational, or technical support to other employees, such as human resources professionals, IT support staff and administrative assistants.

4. **Skilled professionals:**

   Skilled professionals are employees who have specialized knowledge and expertise in a particular field, such as engineers, scientists, and accountants.

5. **Unskilled laborers:**

   Unskilled laborers are employees who perform manual labor or other tasks that do not require specialized knowledge or skills.

Each type of employee plays a critical role in the success of the organization, and it is important for organizations to understand and effectively manage their employees in order to ensure that they are motivated, engaged, and working towards the common goals of the company. This can involve providing adequate compensation and benefits, creating a supportive and positive work environment, and investing in employee development and training programs.

Making Employees Productive

Making employees productive is a critical aspect of organizational success, and it requires a combination of several key strategies:

Provide clear expectations

Employees perform best when they understand exactly what is expected of them. Organizations can provide clear expectations by setting goals, providing clear job descriptions, and communicating regularly with employees about their performance.

Encourage continuous learning and development

Employees who feel that they are growing and developing professionally are more likely to be engaged and motivated at work. Organizations can encourage this by offering training and development programs, mentorship opportunities, and other ways for employees to acquire new skills and knowledge.

Foster a positive work environment: A supportive and positive work environment can help to increase employee motivation, engagement, and performance. Organizations can create a positive work environment by promoting open and honest communication, providing opportunities for employee recognition and feedback, and creating a supportive and inclusive culture.

Provide adequate resources

Employees who have the resources they need to do their jobs effectively are more likely to be productive.

Organizations can provide adequate resources by investing in technology and equipment, providing necessary training, and ensuring that employees have access to the information they need to do their jobs.

Encourage work-life balance

Employees who have a good work-life balance are more likely to be productive and engaged at work. Organizations can encourage work-life balance by offering flexible work arrangements, encouraging employees to take breaks, and promoting a culture of health and well-being.

By implementing these strategies, organizations can create an environment that fosters employee productivity and success. However, it's important to remember that productivity is not just about working harder and longer but also about working smarter and more efficiently, and that requires a holistic approach that takes into account the well-being and satisfaction of employees.

Tools & Equipment

A tool is an instrument that increases an employee's ability to do work. Over the years, the development of tools moved from simple to complex. Whether muscle-powered or mechanically powered, manual or automatic, technology-based, intelligence-based, physical, or process-based system, whatever your people are using to create output.

The evolution of tools has greatly impacted the way work is done. From manual labor to automated systems, the development of tools has made work more efficient, safe, and cost-effective. The invention of new tools and technologies has allowed organizations to increase productivity, reduce waste, and improve the overall quality of their products and services.

For example, the invention of computers and software has revolutionized the way we work, allowing us to automate many tasks, improve communication and collaboration, and store and analyze large amounts of data. Similarly, the development of advanced manufacturing technologies has allowed companies to increase production and improve the quality of their products.

In today's rapidly changing work environment, it is important for organizations to continuously invest in new tools and technologies to stay competitive and meet the demands of their customers.

By investing in tools that increase employee ability to do work, organizations can improve their bottom line while also creating a more enjoyable and fulfilling work environment for their employees.

Tools and equipment can be used to improve efficiency in many ways, including:

1. **Automation:**

   Automation tools and equipment can be used to automate repetitive or time-consuming tasks, freeing up employees to focus on higher-level tasks that require more skill and creativity.

2. **Streamlining processes:**

   Tools and equipment can be used to streamline work processes, reducing the time and resources required to complete tasks and increasing overall efficiency.

3. **Improved productivity:**

   By providing employees with the tools and equipment they need to do their jobs effectively, organizations can increase employee productivity and performance.

4. **Improved safety:**

   The use of safety equipment and tools can help to reduce the risk of workplace injuries and accidents, improving overall efficiency by reducing the need for time off work and healthcare costs.

5. **Enhanced quality:**

   Tools and equipment that are designed to improve the quality of products or services can help organizations increase efficiency by reducing the need for rework and ensuring that products are produced to a high standard.

6. **Increased flexibility:**

   Tools and equipment that are designed to be flexible and adaptable can help organizations to respond quickly to changes in demand or market conditions, increasing efficiency and improving competitiveness.

Tools and equipment play a critical role in improving efficiency in the workplace. By investing in the right tools and equipment, organizations can increase productivity, reduce waste, and improve the quality of their products and services, ultimately driving success and growth.

Manufacturers need to identify the right technological tools that will enable them to come up with business plans effectively and manage their inventories and workflows seamlessly.

Section 3
Speeding up the Work Environment

Training

Training employees is an ongoing process that should be integrated into the daily operations of an organization. Employees are not only a valuable asset but also an investment that requires continuous development and improvement. The continuously changing work environment, new technologies, and shifting market demands all make continuous training a necessity.

By providing ongoing training, organizations can help their employees to:

1. Acquire new skills and knowledge that are relevant to their work and essential to the organization's success.
2. Stay up to date with the latest industry trends and developments, allowing them to stay ahead of the competition.
3. Improve their performance and productivity, helping them achieve their personal and professional goals.
4. Stay motivated and engaged, as they feel valued and supported by the organization.
5. Adapt to changes in the work environment, such as new technologies, processes, or regulations.

Overall, providing ongoing training to employees is an investment in the future success of the organization.

By continuously developing the skills and knowledge of employees, organizations can remain competitive and maintain their position as leaders in their industry.

There are many types of employee training, including On-the-job training:

This type of training involves employees learning new skills and knowledge by working alongside experienced colleagues who provide guidance and feedback.

1. **Classroom training:**

   This type of training involves employees attending structured classes or workshops, where they learn new skills and knowledge from experienced trainers.

2. **Online training:**

   This type of training involves employees accessing training materials and courses online, such as e-learning modules, webinars, or video tutorials.

3. **Simulation training:**

   This type of training involves employees using simulations or virtual reality environments to practice new skills in a safe and controlled environment.

4. **Mentorship programs:**

   This type of training involves employees being paired with experienced mentors who provide guidance and support as they learn new skills and knowledge.

5. **Coaching and feedback:**

   This type of training involves employees receiving one-on-one coaching and feedback from their manager or a designated coach, aimed at helping them improve their performance.

6. **Cross-training:**

   This type of training involves employees learning new skills and knowledge in areas outside their regular job responsibilities, helping them become more versatile and valuable to the organization.

   The type of training that is best suited to an organization and its employees will depend on a range of factors, including the nature of the work, the skills and knowledge required, and the learning preferences of employees. By offering a range of training options, organizations can ensure that they meet the needs of all employees and provide them with the skills and knowledge they need to succeed.

Communication

Strategic communication that engages employees in the company's purpose, mission and values can increase the speed at which an organization achieves its goals. It can educate, motivate, inspire and increase employee engagement.

When employees understand and buy into a company's purpose, mission, and values, they are more likely to be motivated and engaged in their work. This can lead to improved productivity, better job satisfaction, and a more positive work environment. Additionally, clear and effective communication of a company's goals and objectives can help align employees and create a shared sense of purpose, which can drive progress towards achieving those goals.

High employee engagement leads to better customer experience, productivity, retention, and profitability, which are all metrics that affect an organization's success.

However, it's important for communication to be strategic and not just a one-time event. Companies need to make sure that their purpose, mission, and values are woven into all aspects of their operations and that they are consistently communicated and reinforced to employees. This can be done through regular town hall meetings, training programs, performance evaluations, and other channels of communication.

In a nutshell, strategic communication is an important tool for organizations to engage employees and drive progress towards their goals.

Improving communication within an organization may lead to increased collaboration, better decision-making, and improved job satisfaction. Here are some steps organizations can take to improve communication:

1. **Open and transparent channels of communication:**

   Encourage employees to share their ideas and concerns and ensure that all employees have access to the information they need to do their jobs effectively.

2. **Encourage active listening:**

   Foster a culture of active listening, where employees feel heard and valued. This can be done by providing training and resources on effective communication, and by setting aside dedicated time for employees to discuss their concerns and ideas.

3. **Promote clear and concise messaging:**

   Make sure that messages are clear and concise, and that all employees understand the information that is being communicated. This can be done by using simple language, avoiding jargon, and providing visual aids such as charts and diagrams.

4. **Foster collaboration and teamwork:**

   Encourage employees to work together and share ideas. This can be done by creating cross-functional teams, holding regular team-building activities, and encouraging collaboration through tools like instant messaging and video conferencing.

5. **Encourage feedback:**

   Encourage employees to provide feedback on their experiences with communication and use this feedback to make improvements. Create forums where employees can provide feedback and suggestions on communication and collaboration within the organization.

6. **Use technology effectively:**

   Utilize technology to improve communication, such as video conferencing, instant messaging, and collaboration tools.

7. **Lead by example:**

   Managers and leaders can play a key role in improving communication by modelling effective communication skills and being open to feedback from employees.

8. **Gamification:**

   Use games and other fun activities to engage employees and encourage communication. This can include team-building exercises, scavenger hunts, and other interactive activities.

9. **Social media:**

   Utilize social media platforms like Facebook, Twitter, and LinkedIn to connect employees and promote communication and collaboration.

10. Virtual reality:

Use virtual reality to simulate real-life scenarios, such as team-building activities, and encourage employees to collaborate and communicate in a virtual environment.

11. Employee advocacy:

Encourage employees to become ambassadors for the organization, sharing information about the company, its products, and its mission on social media and other channels.

12. Employee-generated content:

Encourage employees to create and share content that promotes the company's mission and values, such as blog posts, videos, and infographics.

13. Internal chatbots:

Implement chatbots that can assist employees with information and support, freeing up time for face-to-face communication and collaboration.

Integration

Integrating disparate systems can greatly improve productivity within an organization. Disparate systems refer to separate systems or software that are used by different departments or teams within an organization but are not integrated with each other. This can lead to inefficiencies, duplication of work, and data silos.By integrating these incongruent systems, an organization can streamline processes, reduce errors, and increase visibility into data and operations. For example, integrating an organization's financial, and customer relationship management (CRM) and human resources (HR) systems can provide a more complete and accurate view of the organization's data and operations.

Additionally, integrating systems can automate manual processes and increase the speed at which work can be completed, freeing up employees to focus on higher-value tasks.

Often, employees of manufacturing firms spend considerable time switching between various systems to perform different tasks. This affects their performance adversely; a study reveals switching systems to perform multiple tasks could reduce productivity by as much as 40%. This problem is more pronounced with companies which have acquired other organizations. Employees of these firms need to deal with multiple systems at the backend. The problems with disparate systems can be reduced by integrating them.

Here's an interesting success story that explains how I helped a company eliminate the need for multiple systems using ERP.

A manufacturing company was using multiple systems to manage their operations, including separate systems for inventory management, accounting, and production planning. This led to inefficiencies and errors, as data had to be manually entered into each system and was not always up-to-date.

I was approached to assess the company's operations and recommend solutions. After conducting a thorough analysis, I recommended the implementation of an ERP system to integrate all of the company's disparate systems into one centralized platform.

The ERP system was implemented and configured to meet the specific needs of the company. This allowed the company to streamline processes, automate manual tasks, and provide real-time visibility into its operations. The company was able to eliminate the need for multiple systems, and all of its operations were managed through the ERP platform.

As a result of the implementation, the company experienced improved efficiency and accuracy in its operations, and its employees were able to focus on higher-value tasks. Additionally, the company was able to make informed decisions based on real-time data and insights, leading to increased revenue and improved customer satisfaction.

I was able to help the company eliminate the need for multiple systems and improve its operations by recommending and implementing an ERP system. The ERP system provided a centralized platform for all of the company's operations and allowed for improved efficiency, accuracy, and decision-making.

Section 4
Enhancing Effectiveness of the Work Environment

Cycle-Time Review

Cycle-time review is a process improvement method that helps to increase productivity by reducing the time it takes to complete a task or process. The goal of the cycle-time review is to identify bottlenecks and inefficiencies in a process and make improvements to reduce the cycle time or the time it takes to complete a process from start to finish.

Usually, an organization's cost and efficiency are associated with the time duration it takes to repeat the same process or unit of output again & again. Cycle time review focuses on calculating and improving the operational performance of the business. To take a leap ahead of their competition, manufacturers need to find ways to reduce production time and cost to improve operating performance and Product quality.

If the reduction in cycle time is fifty per cent and work in process inventory turns twice, it causes output to increase from twenty to seventy per cent. As output increases, resource capacity is freed. Two major effects take place: expenses turn down, and the manufacturing firm becomes capable of producing considerably more output with fewer assets.

Here's how cycle-time review can help increase productivity:

1. **Identifies bottlenecks:**

   By analysing the time it takes to complete each step in a process, the cycle-time review can identify bottlenecks and areas where time is being wasted.

2. **Improves process flow:**

   By removing bottlenecks and inefficiencies, the cycle-time review can improve the flow of a process, reducing the time it takes to complete a task.

3. **Increases efficiency:**

   By streamlining processes and reducing cycle time, cycle-time review can increase overall efficiency and productivity.

4. **Improves quality:**

   By reducing the time it takes to complete a task, cycle-time review can also help improve the quality of the output, as there is less room for error.

5. **Increases employee satisfaction:**

   By streamlining processes and reducing cycle time, cycle-time review can also increase employee satisfaction, as employees are able to complete tasks more quickly and efficiently.

Cycle-time reviews can be implemented through the following steps:

1. **Define the process:**

   The first step in implementing the cycle-time review is to define the process that will be analyzed. This could be a single task or a larger process that involves multiple steps.

2. **Gather data:**

   Next, data needs to be gathered on the process. This includes the time it takes to complete each step in the process, the number of steps involved, and any bottlenecks or inefficiencies that are present.

3. **analyze the data:**

   Once the data has been gathered, it can be analyzed to identify areas where time is being wasted and where improvements can be made. This may involve creating a flowchart of the process, mapping out the time it takes to complete each step, and identifying bottlenecks and inefficiencies.

4. **Make improvements:**

   Based on the analysis, improvements can be made to reduce cycle time and improve the flow of the process. This may involve removing steps that are not necessary, streamlining processes, or automating tasks.

5. **Implement changes:**

   Once the improvements have been identified, they need to be implemented. This may involve training employees on new processes, updating systems and software, or making changes to physical processes.

6. Monitor and measure:

Finally, it is important to monitor and measure the results of the cycle-time review. This involves tracking the cycle time after the changes have been made and comparing it to the original cycle time. If the changes have not had the desired effect, further improvements can be made.

Fair implementation of cycle-time review; can reduce cycle time and improve the flow of their processes, leading to increased efficiency and productivity.

Process Performance Monitoring

Process performance monitoring refers to the ongoing measurement and evaluation of key performance indicators (KPIs) to determine the efficiency and effectiveness of business processes. It is an important tool for organizations to improve their operational performance and achieve their goals.

Business needs to evolve constantly, and organizational processes must enable companies to meet their needs. Manufacturers need to review their processes at regular intervals to identify lacunae and take appropriate steps to improve them.

Ask the following questions before making changes to an existing process.

1. What is the time consumed by the process? Can it be completed faster? If so, how?
2. What are the tools needed by personnel to complete the process successfully? How much do they cost?
3. What can be done to complete the process at a lower cost? It's advisable to embark on a process upgrade only when it results in a substantial financial benefit. Here are a few steps to implement process performance monitoring:

1. **Define the process:**

   The first step is to clearly define the process that will be monitored. This could be a single task or a larger process that involves multiple steps.

2. **Identify key performance indicators:**

   Next, identify the KPIs that will be used to monitor the process. These KPIs should be relevant to the process, measurable, and aligned with the organization's goals.

3. **Set targets:**

   Once the KPIs have been identified, set targets for each one. These targets should be specific, measurable, and achievable and should reflect the desired level of performance for the process.

4. **Gather data:**

   To monitor process performance, data must be gathered on the KPIs. This may involve using software tools to automate data collection or manually collecting data through surveys, audits, or other methods.

5. **Analyze the data:**

   The data should be analyzed to determine whether the process is meeting its targets. This may involve creating charts, graphs, or other visual representations to help understand the data.

6. **Act:**

   Based on the analysis, decisions should be made about what actions to take to improve process performance.

This may involve making changes to the process, providing additional training to employees, or investing in new technology.

7. **Continuously monitor and adjust:**

   Finally, process performance should be monitored on an ongoing basis to ensure that the process remains efficient and effective over time. This may involve repeating the process performance monitoring cycle on a regular basis and making adjustments as needed.

Section 5

Assessment and Implementation

Issue Discovery

Knowing the issues and your immediate focus area in a manufacturing plant is extremely important. **Early detection and precise area identification of problems make your efforts more effective.**

Additionally, identifying and addressing issues can improve the quality of the products being produced, helping to maintain the reputation of the company and ensure customer satisfaction.

Working on efficiency shall automatically reduce the issues related to other common problems, such as equipment breakdowns, product defects, and even safety hazards.

By implementing the "Efficiency Step-up Blueprint", companies can stay ahead of potential problems and keep their manufacturing operations running smoothly.

I have identified some Quick Questions to Assess the efficiency issues of your Manufacturing Plant.

These are only indicative questions, and you may develop and frame more like these.

1. Are production schedules consistently being met?
2. Is there a high rate of equipment breakdowns or malfunctions?
3. Are there bottlenecks in the production process that are causing delays?

4. Are there requent quality control issues with products?
5. Is there excessive waste or scrap generated during production?
6. Are raw materials being used efficiently, or is there a high rate of spoilage or waste?
7. Is energy consumption higher than expected for the level of production?
8. Are employees reporting inefficiencies or difficulties with equipment or processes?
9. Arc thoro long wait times for necessary supplies or materials?
10. Are there regular maintenance issues with equipment or machinery?
11. Are machines and equipment regularly maintained and serviced?
12. Is there a regular process in place for monitoring and tracking equipment performance?
13. Are employees trained on the proper use of equipment and processes?
14. Is there a clear process in place for reporting and addressing issues?
15. Are inventory levels and raw material usage being monitored effectively?
16. Are there any bottlenecks in the production process that slow down production?
17. Are energy and resource consumption levels within expected ranges?

18. Are there any areas where waste is being generated unnecessarily?
19. Are there any recurring problems with product quality or defects?
20. Are there any safety concerns or hazards in the workplace?

Answering these questions can provide a good starting point for identifying areas where improvements can be made to increase efficiency and reduce costs in a manufacturing plant.

Further, there are several other methods for assessment & observation that would reveal the efficiency issues.

These are:

1. **Regular Inspections:**

   Regular visual inspections of equipment, machinery, and processes can help identify potential problems early on. This includes checking for wear and tear, leaks, cracks, and any other signs of malfunction.

2. **Maintenance Records:**

   Keeping accurate records of maintenance and repairs can help identify patterns of problems and areas that need improvement. This can also help prevent future breakdowns by identifying parts that need regular replacement.

3. **Employee Feedback:**

   Encouraging employees to report any issues they observe during their work can provide valuable information about potential problems. Employees often have first-hand experience with the equipment and can identify problems that might be missed by management.

4. **Equipment Monitoring:**

   Installing sensors and monitoring equipment to track the performance of machines can provide real-time data on how equipment is functioning. This can help identify potential problems before they become major issues.

5. **Process Audits:**

   Regularly auditing the manufacturing processes can help identify inefficiencies and areas for improvement. This can include reviewing the use of raw materials, energy consumption, and waste generation.

6. **Quality Control:**

   Implementing a strong quality control program can help identify problems with products and processes before they become major issues. This includes regular testing and inspections of products, as well as analysing data from production runs.

Overall, a combination of these methods can provide a comprehensive approach to discovering and addressing issues in a manufacturing plant.

Power Principles

Implementing a strategy in business can be challenging however, I have developed 5 Power Principles that can help you to ensure success in implementing. Here are some rules to consider when implementing a strategy in business:

Rule 1: Understand Your Numbers

Monitoring the Parameters

Understanding your key numbers is a critical component of effective business management, strategic implementation and improving efficiency. Without proper understanding of your performance parameters, you cannot monitor the status of implementation or even assess the effectiveness of the strategies implemented so far.

Numbers are not necessarily expected only to be financial, but non-financial parameters should also be collected, analyzed and co-related with financial numbers. Such as worker's ease, time and motion data, operational metrics, and quantitative & qualitative numbers, among others. These non-financial parameters can provide important insights into your business performance and can help you identify areas for improvement.

For example, monitoring employee engagement can help you identify opportunities to improve your workplace culture and increase productivity. By analyzing operational metrics, such as production efficiency or sales conversion rates, you can identify areas where you can improve processes and drive better results.

By tracking both financial and non-financial parameters, you can get a more complete picture of your business Process Performance and make data-driven decisions that drive success and growth for your company.

Rule 2: Excellence is the only Acceptable Performance Target

Cause & Effect Analysis

Setting a target of excellence as the only acceptable performance level is a powerful approach to driving results in a business. The concept of "excellence as the only acceptable target" means that you strive for the highest possible level of performance in every aspect of your business, and are never satisfied with mediocrity or complacency.

Cause-and-effect analysis can be a helpful tool in achieving this target of excellence. This approach involves systematically identifying the root causes of problems and challenges, and implementing solutions to address those causes. By focusing on the underlying causes of performance issues, rather than just addressing the symptoms, you can achieve more sustainable and lasting results.

For example, if you're experiencing low sales, a cause-and-effect analysis might help you identify factors such as a lack of product differentiation, ineffective marketing efforts, or poor customer service, among others. By addressing the root causes of these issues, you can improve your sales performance and achieve the target of excellence.

By consistently striving for excellence and using cause-and-effect analysis to address performance issues, you can drive continuous improvement and create a culture of high performance in your business.

Rule 3: Knowledge-Driven Environment

Communicate Extra-Ordinarily

A knowledge-driven environment is one in which information and learning are highly valued and continuously pursued. This type of environment fosters creativity, innovation, and continuous improvement, and is critical for staying ahead in today's fast-paced, competitive business landscape.

Communicating effectively is an important part of creating and maintaining a knowledge-driven environment.

This means not only sharing information and insights, but also actively seeking out new ideas and perspectives, and encouraging open and honest dialogue.

To communicate extra-ordinarily in a knowledge-driven environment, it's important to

1. **Encourage open communication:**

   Create a culture where all voices are heard, and employees feel comfortable sharing their ideas and opinions.

2. **Foster collaboration:**

   Encourage employees to work together and share their knowledge and expertise to drive better results.

3. **Embrace new technologies:**

   Use technology and digital tools to share information, collaborate, and access knowledge from a wide range of sources.

4. **Invest in learning and development:**

   Provide opportunities for employees to develop their skills and acquire new knowledge and recognize and reward those who demonstrate a commitment to continuous learning.

By fostering a culture of continuous learning and effective communication, you can create a knowledge-driven environment that drives innovation, improves performance, and helps you stay ahead in your industry.

Rule 4: Keep Processes Simple

Easy to Understand, Simple to Follow

Keeping processes simple is a key principle of effective business operations. Simple processes are easier to understand and follow, which can lead to improved efficiency, higher levels of employee engagement, and reduced errors and mistakes.

Here are a few tips for keeping processes simple:

1. **Identify the purpose:**

   Clearly define the purpose and desired outcomes of each process, and ensure that it is aligned with your overall business goals.

2. **Streamline steps:**

   Eliminate unnecessary steps and simplify processes wherever possible. The fewer steps involved, the easier it will be for employees to understand and follow.

3. **Make it visual:**

   Use diagrams, flow charts, or other visual aids to help employees understand and follow processes.

4. **Use technology:**

   Automate repetitive tasks and use technology to streamline processes and reduce the number of manual steps involved.

5. **Get feedback:**

    Regularly solicit feedback from employees on the processes they use, and use their input to improve and simplify processes over time.

By keeping processes simple and easy to understand, you can improve efficiency, reduce errors and mistakes, and create a more engaged and productive workforce.

Rule 5: Establish Clarity in Leadership & Command

One Point/One Direction Instruction

Clarity in leadership and command refers to the quality of clear and effective communication from a leader to their team. A leader with clarity in their leadership and command is able to articulate their vision, goals, and expectations in a way that is easily understood by their team.

To establish clarity in this area, leaders should focus on providing one-point or one-direction instructions that are concise, specific, and actionable. This helps to ensure that team members have a clear understanding of what is expected of them and what they need to do in order to meet the leader's expectations.

Additionally, leaders should also encourage open communication and feedback from their team so that they can adjust their instructions as needed to ensure that they are effectively communicating their vision and goals.

Developing & Maintaining a Supportive Staff

Here are some steps that can be taken to make staff supportive in a manufacturing plant:

1. **Clear Communication:**

   Regular and transparent communication can help build trust and create a sense of community among employees. This includes clear expectations, regular updates on the company's goals and progress, and open forums for feedback and suggestions.

2. **Employee Involvement:**

   Involving employees in decision-making processes and giving them a voice in the workplace can increase their sense of ownership and commitment to the company. This can be done through regular meetings, suggestion programs, and employee surveys.

3. **Training and Development:**

   Providing opportunities for training and development can help employees feel valued and empowered. This can include training on new technologies, processes, and equipment, as well as leadership and management training.

4. **Recognition and Rewards:**

   Recognizing and rewarding employees for their contributions can boost morale and create a positive work environment. This can include performance bonuses, awards, and promotions, as well as more informal gestures of appreciation, such as verbal recognition or a simple thank you.

5. **Employee Well-being:**

   Fostering a positive work-life balance and promoting employee well-being can help increase job satisfaction and reduce stress and burnout. This can include offering flexible schedules, wellness programs, and a supportive work environment.

6. **Empowerment:**

   Allowing employees to take on new challenges and responsibilities can increase their sense of ownership and commitment to their work. This can include giving employees the authority to make decisions, taking on new projects, and being part of cross-functional teams.

By implementing these steps, companies can create a supportive work environment that helps employees feel valued and engaged and encourages them to work together to achieve common goals.

Mindset & Belief Alignment with Goals & Objectives

Mindset and belief play a critical role in the success of an entrepreneur. A positive and growth-oriented mindset can help entrepreneurs overcome challenges and pursue their goals with determination and resilience.

Here are some key aspects of a successful entrepreneur's mindset and belief system:

1. **A Growth Mindset:**

   Having a growth mindset means believing that one's abilities and intelligence can be developed through effort and experience. This mindset can help entrepreneurs approach challenges and failures as opportunities for growth and learning.

2. **Positive Thinking:**

   Entrepreneurs with a positive outlook are more likely to see opportunities and find solutions to problems. Positive thinking can also help entrepreneurs maintain their motivation and energy levels, even in the face of setbacks.

3. **Resilience:**

   Resilience is the ability to bounce back from failure and adversity. Entrepreneurs with a strong sense of resilience can handle setbacks and keep moving forward, even when things get tough.

4. **Confidence:**

   Confidence in oneself and one's abilities can help entrepreneurs take calculated risks and pursue their goals with determination. This confidence can also help entrepreneurs communicate their vision and inspire others to believe in their ideas.

5. **Vision and Purpose:**

   Having a clear vision and a sense of purpose can help entrepreneurs stay focused and motivated. This can include a vision for thc futuro of their company, as well as a deeper understanding of why their work is important and meaningful.

   By developing a growth-oriented mindset, positive thinking, resilience, confidence, and a clear sense of purpose, entrepreneurs can set themselves up for success and overcome the challenges that come with building a business.

   Aligning mindset and belief with the goals of a business is also important for an entrepreneur to achieve success and overcome challenges. Here are some steps to help align mindset and belief with business goals:

6. **Identify your goals:**

   Start by defining your business goals, both in the short-term and long-term. This can include specific targets for growth, revenue, and market share, as well as broader goals related to your company's purpose and impact.

7. **Assess your mindset:**

   Take some time to reflect on your current mindset and belief system. Are you confident, resilient, and growth-oriented, or do you tend to focus on setbacks and limitations? Understanding your current mindset can help you identify areas for improvement.

8. **Create a positive vision:**

   Use your goals as a starting point to create a positive vision for the future of your business. Visualize your company succeeding and reaching its goals, and imagine the impact that this success will have on your life and the lives of others.

9. **Adopt a growth mindset:**

   Embrace a growth mindset by focusing on learning and improvement rather than just results. Approach challenges and failures as opportunities for growth and learning and celebrate your progress and successes along the way.

10. **Cultivate resilience:**

    Build resilience by learning from failures and setbacks, and by seeking out new challenges and opportunities. Develop a positive and optimistic outlook and focus on finding solutions rather than dwelling on problems.

11. Cultivate self-awareness:

Regularly take time to reflect on your thoughts, feelings, and actions, and seek out feedback from others. This self-awareness can help you identify areas where you may need to change your beliefs or behaviors in order to align with your business goals.

By following these steps, entrepreneurs can align their mindset and belief system with the goals of their business and increase their chances of success and fulfilment.

Section 6
Case Studies

Case Study 1

The Manufacturing Unit

A factory manufacturing seats for two-wheeler bikes.

The Challenge

In the process of making a saddle, they needed to manufacture foams. Foam making was not a very complex process, **but the manufacturing unit was using a specific chemical component almost double the standard quantity.**

The Solution

This is how we identified and resolved the issue and reduced costs to a significant level.

We started by observing the process and noting down the different motions on the shop floor with the time chunk involved in each motion.

Through a careful observation process, we realised in a few days that which material element was being used excessively than the standard consumption.

It was the release agent that was being consumed in almost double the quantum of standard consumption.

However, the real challenge started thereafter because the reason for the excess usage of material was unknown.

Even after several days of observation & analysis, the material usage could not be improved.

Whenever we tried adjusting the application of this chemical, the piece started to stick with the mould, and again we had to use the previous setting.

After careful study and dedicated efforts, we succeeded in knowing the reason behind the over-usage.

We concluded that the labors on the line were using a cloth piece to wipe the moulds clean and while wiping, the grease from the mould, the previous pieces were also removed, and hence each new piece required additional usages. We simply stopped wiping the moulds after the production of each piece.

The Amazing Efficiency Step-up Results

By doing this, we **saved 9 manpower on 3 assembly lines and 3 shifts. 24 Liters of chemical usage each day, usage of cloths and also fastened the process by 12** seconds.

This apparently simple efficiency intervention not only **saved 18 lakhs annually, it also resulted in a 3% increase in productivity.**

Case Study 2

The Manufacturing Unit

Let's see another incident where one of my mentees was producing cycle frames.

The Challenge

I noticed that the **production process was producing a high number of defective joints** that either had to be thrown away or had to be reworked.

To reduce the amount of waste, we took the following steps:

The Solution

We conducted a root cause analysis that involved investigating the underlying reasons why the joints were defective. We looked at factors such as the raw materials being used, the production process itself, and the equipment being used.

Based on our findings from the root cause analysis, **we made changes to the production process to improve the quality of the frame joints and reduce the number of defects.**

For example, we **introduced new quality control checks** so that each frame pipe and head bracket or bottom bracket was sent for welding only after thorough check for smooth corners. We **issued an altogether new** checklist for welding.

We also **adjusted the production equipment to produce more accurate results.** We started a process of **employee training for employees on the new process improvements to ensure that they were aware of the changes and could implement them correctly.**

After implementing the changes, we started monitoring the results and evaluated the impact we had on reducing waste.

The Amazing Efficiency Step-up Result

The process improvements and quality checks finally resulted in negligible wastage and had an impact of a **significant 7% less cost of manufacturing.**

Case Study 3

The Manufacturing Unit

A manufacturing company producing inverters.

The Challenge

The company was facing a challenge with low production rates, resulting in delayed deliveries and frustrated customers.

To increase production, the company decided to implement a Lean Manufacturing process. The following steps were taken:

The Solution

We conducted a value stream mapping analysis. **This involved mapping out the entire production process to identify areas of waste and inefficiency.** The analysis showed that **there were several bottlenecks in the process that were slowing down production.**

We **implemented a system of continuous improvement (Kaizen)** based on the value stream mapping analysis. The company identified several areas where improvements could be made to increase production. **They introduced new tools and equipment to streamline the production process, such**

as automation and robotics, and implemented a **5S system to keep the workspace organized and efficient.**

The company also involved employees in the improvement process, seeking their input on how to increase production and making changes based on their suggestions. This helped to create a sense of ownership among employees and encouraged them to work towards the common goal of increasing production.

The **company further established key performance indicators (KPIs) to track production rates and measure the success of their efforts.** By regularly monitoring these KPIs, they were able to identify areas where further improvements could be made.

The Amazing Efficiency Step-up Results

As a result of these efforts, the company saw a **significant increase in production rates.** They were able to **deliver products to customers faster and improve their overall customer satisfaction.** The company's success in **increasing production through Lean Manufacturing helped to establish them as a leader in their industry.**

Section 7

The Ways Ahead

Recap

Just 3 Aspects to Efficiency

1. Create an Ideal Work Environment

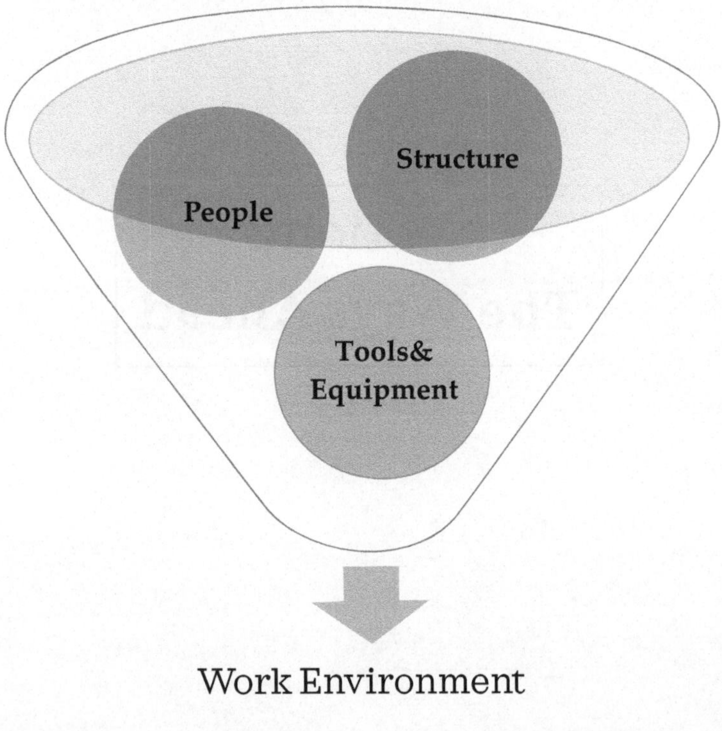

2. Speed up the Work Environment

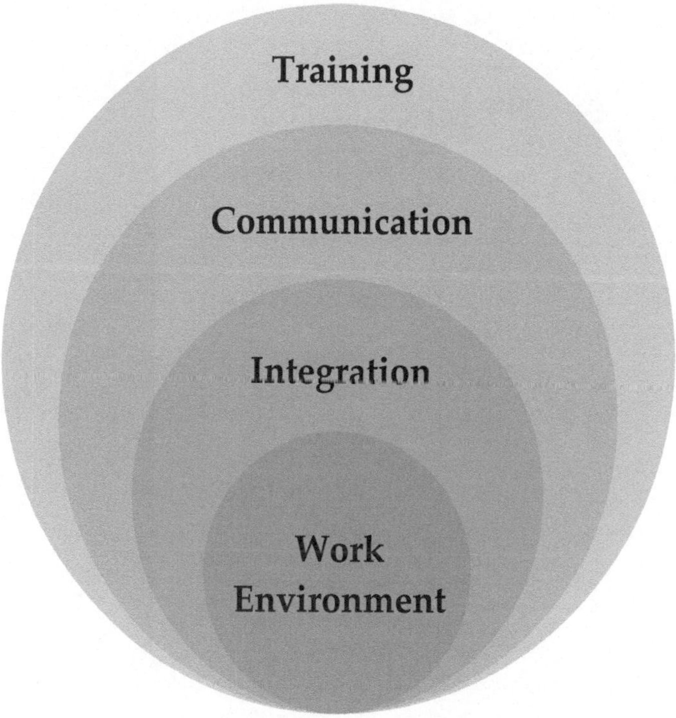

3. Enhance Effectiveness of the Work Environment

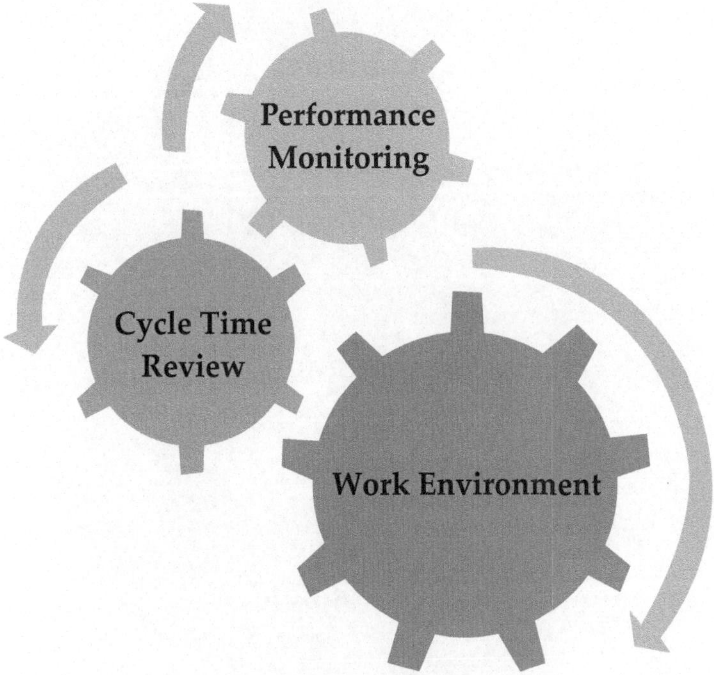

Say aloud, **"I am making this company super- efficient".**

Implement this blueprint following the '3C' Principles

a. Consistency

b. Clarity and

c. Commitment

And Remember the 5 Power Principles of Implementation

Rule 1 : Understand Your Numbers (Monitoring the Parameters)

Rule 2 : Excellence is the only Acceptable Performance Target (Cause & Effect Analysis)

Rule 3 : A Knowledge-Driven Environment (Communicate Extra-Ordinarily)

Rule 4 : Keep Processes Simple (Easy to Understand, Simple to Follow)

Rule 5 : Establish Clarity in Leadership & Command (One Point/ One Direction Instruction)

Go ahead with confidence

Choices

You have the complete knowledge of the Rules to Rule in Business right here in this book and you also have my full support. You can go ahead and implement these on your own in the following 5 easy steps:

Steps to Implement

1. Make up your Mind
2. Draft a Strategy
3. Appoint a process implementor
4. Make a review rhythm
5. Modify strategy if required

Result requires your intent, efforts and time and I am sure that you will succeed, sooner or later.

Reach out to me for all your queries/doubts or explanations needed. With no cost involved on your part.

Mail me: jai@jaisethi.com

OR

If you wish to turbo-charge the transformation of your business at super-sonic speed, You can have me by your side—hand holding you through the entire process...

My team can work in sync with your team to win together in a sure-shot manner sticking to the mutually decided speediest timeline possible. The choice is yours— I am with you either way.

What to do next

It's time, and you know it.

You and your team (for some cases, my team also) have identified the idea that will change your world and results. It will be a game-changer for you. It is big, it is bold, and it is not like anything you have tried before.

You've implemented ideas before, but nothing this important or big. So, obviously, you are excited and a bit scared; but you know it is time to act.

Here are the things you can take on, to improve the chances that your big idea becomes a big success.

The processes have already been thought through in your mind. Start with baby steps. First, ensure your overheads and any risky thing is under control. Once you are in the safe zone, then migrate slowly. Use the 80-20 rule. Spend more time with the current model and then 20% time on new changes that you've planned.

Solve broken links first and then identify someone from the team and give charge. This, too, will happen slowly. Don't take sudden action.

Strategy implementation is vital for moving a company forward. Wherever a business fails to implement and execute its strategies properly, it simply fails to move forward and grow. Implementation is the process of executing a plan or policy so that a concept becomes a reality. Whether a business is a start-up or well-established, implementation of a well-thought-out strategy is a major challenge in front of the management.

Knowledge doesn't make much of a difference in our life. Consider this, we all know how to reduce/gain weight, but still, 90% of us are unable to be our desired weight— we are either overweight or underweight.

Content has become a commodity nowadays. You can acquire knowledge by just paying a few bucks but cannot reap its benefits without flawless execution of the same.

Knowing that what to do or even how to do is one thing, and getting it implemented is an entirely different thing.

What I have learned during my consulting career and while working with various businesses in strategic implementation and also realized while working on my own business growth journey is that there are no specific formulae that fit all. However, all those businesses that grew had a great implementation mechanism and tremendous speed of execution.

"Knowledge is not power; Implementation is power."

Garrison Wynn

Keep the fire burning and stay in touch with people who motivate you and your team to be on the right path... And you will succeed... The Game of Efficiency is not merely about the end but a process of improving every day.

The Author

CA Jai Sethi

FCA, ISA (ICA), DIPL (ILI),
DBM (UK), B. Com.

- Chartered Accountant
- Internal Control Expert
- Financial Literacy Coach
- Registered Independent Director
- Corporate Trainer, Speaker, Author
- Internal Auditor to over 60 Companies
- Inventor of the "Efficiency Step-up Blueprint"
- Management & Business Growth Consultant

PROFILE SUMMARY

Author's Note

As a mentor to over 1000 entrepreneurs, and a highly motivated speaker, corporate trainer & business consultant with 18+ years of professional experience in consulting & training small and medium groups across diverse industries; I understood that entrepreneurs are constantly searching for a facilitator & an expert who may help them and their organization explore and achieve their true potential and can guide and mentor them to become an efficient brand on the path to growth and prosperity.

Based on my research, experience and learnings of many years, I not only coach & mentor entrepreneurs but also run orientation programmes for your team of executives (top-level & middle-level) so that they can be versed with and can well appreciate the corporate goals and stay aligned with the organizational position, their job expectations, and can contribute to the success of the organization.

It is also crucial that your team should also be versed with the financial reports they are generating, receiving or responsible for. To facilitate this, I have a proven track of success in leveraging financial & business decision theories and methodologies to design, develop, and deliver successful training programs and integrate instructional technology to provide onsite and virtual training.

I'm also adept at and focus on organizing and facilitating "Finance for non- finance" training in various corporates to increase the financial literacy of the overall team.

MY VISION & MISSION

I'm an Efficiency Architect; I help businesses improve operational efficiency & processes in businesses; I'm the founder of the Successpreneurs Hub, and

I am on a MISSION of creating 1 million impactful brands that are known for "Giving High Value at Optimized Costs"; brands that are scalable and creating wealth for all their stakeholders.

That's why I have created the "Efficiency Step-up Blueprint"

I also aspire to make executives versed with and make them appreciate the corporate expectations, financial documents & reports to turn them into major contributors to the advancement of corporate goals & their Job expectations.

With more than 15 years of experience as a Chartered Accountant & Business Consultant, my core strength lies f in delivering skill development of executives in various group sizes with creative communication & development. Equipped with exceptional critical and analytical thinking skills, I excel at:

- Delivering Management Systems
- Process Improvements
- Individual and Group Instruction
- Learning assessment

That can catapult any organization to step-up its efficiency operations.

Internal Control Systems in organizations

Other Books

Accounting & Business Decisions (2015)

A comprehensive Hand Book to guide you to take Smart Business Decisions, using your Accounting Numbers & Contextual Factors

Decision making is critical to entrepreneurs & needed at every function of Management. Every day, you have to set out on a course of action, choose tactics, evaluate results, and otherwise choose from arrays of options.

How do you make decisions in your business?

Are your choices based purely on your gut feelings or on the basis of analytical calculations and a cost-benefit Analysis? Everyone has their own decision-making style, but for the best results, you need to follow a balanced approach.